MINISTRY OF MUNITIONS.

Department of Aircraft Production.

TECHNICAL DEPARTMENT.

I.C. No. 620.

VICTORIA EMBANKMENT,
W.C.2.
Issued March, 1918.

Report on Fokker Triplane.

The following brief report on the Fokker Triplane is issued for information, though it is felt that the machine exhibits few instructive features.

J. G. WEIR,

Lieut.-Colonel,

Controller, Technical Department.

Compiled, 14/3/18

T.5. D.804(R). 19/6/18.

The Naval & Military Press Ltd

Published by
The Naval & Military Press Ltd
5 Riverside, Brambleside, Bellbrook
Industrial Estate, Uckfield, East Sussex,
TN22 1QQ England

Tel: +44 (0) 1825 749494
Fax: +44 (0) 1825 765701

www.naval-military-press.com
www.military-genealogy.com

In reprinting in facsimile from the original, any imperfections are inevitably reproduced and the quality may fall short of modern type and cartographic standards.

MINISTRY OF MUNITIONS.

Department of Aircraft Production.

TECHNICAL DEPARTMENT.

I.C. No. 620.

Victoria Embankment,
W.C.2.
Issued March, 1918.

Report on Fokker Triplane.

The following brief report on the Fokker Triplane is issued for information, though it is felt that the machine exhibits few instructive features.

J. G. Weir,

Lieut.-Colonel,

Controller, Technical Department.

Compiled, 14/3/18

Report on Fokker Triplane.

REPORT ON FOKKER TRIPLANE.

The following report is a brief critical summary of the data obtainable from the Fokker Triplane now in the Aircraft View Rooms, together with such preliminary information as has been received from Expeditionary Force. A fuller report may be issued in the near future, if further enquiry shews that the machine has features of interest. At present, however, the Fokker appears to be one of the poorest of modern German designs.

GENERAL DESCRIPTION.

As regards outline design, the machine is somewhat similar to the Sopwith Triplane and is in general of orthodox type.

The chief point which arises from a preliminary examination is:—

The absence of external bracing wires.

This point will be dealt with later.

The photographs and drawings (Figures 1 to 5) give a good idea of the general arrangement.

CONSTRUCTIONAL DESIGN.

It is from this standpoint, probably, that the machine is of greatest interest. The designer appears to have made every effort to reduce head resistance, even at the expense of increase in weight. In some respects, also, his efforts have tended to grave structural weakness.

WING STRUCTURE.

The unique " twin " spar is shown in Fig. 5. It consists of two box-section tapering spars joined by transverse ply-wood. As far as can be gathered at present, the fore and aft shear strength of this built-up member is supplied by one port and one starboard bulkhead of ply-wood in each plane. This appears quite inadequate, especially in a high speed machine, even if we disregard the possibility of buckling of the laterally-unstabilized ply-wood in nosediving.

Apart from this point, the internal wing structure presents no peculiarities. From the front spar to the leading edge, the upper surface is stiffened with ply-wood as is usual on many modern scouts.

The nature of the main cellule structure is a typical example of the high price paid for reduction of resistance. Interplane wiring is dispensed with, and structurally the main frame may be regarded as three pairs of cantilevers, tied by pseudo-struts near the wing tips.

On a machine of relatively short span this cantilever construction may be rendered possible by the use of spars of great depth, and the ply-wood box type spars employed meet this condition, owing to the abnormally high thickness-chord ratio of the aerofoil section. It is questionable whether the gain in overall efficiency by deletion of bracing wires is sufficient to balance the loss due to the use of a " high lift " section; this question naturally becomes more acute at high speeds, especially when at altitudes not approaching the ceiling; it is also rendered acute by the abnormally small gap-chord ratio employed.

The function of the interplane " struts " appears to be that of ties which partially distribute the load from plane to plane. Their section is such that they can hardly be expected to withstand reverse loading, and it is thought that this fact may be one explanation of the bad name which the Fokker has earned by breakage in the air.

TAIL UNIT STRUCTURE.

Here again we find that reduction of resistance has been attained by deletion of external bracing. In this case, however, the tail unit being largely of tubular construction, the cantilever structure, beside being heavy, is very weak. The proportions of the framework are approximately such as obtain on most normally-braced frameworks, and once more an explanation suggests itself for the structural failures experienced on this type.

FUSELAGE STRUCTURE.

The framework of the fuselage is built-up from steel tubing butt-welded at the joints. The standard wiring attachments consist of a short length of small tubing bent to the form of a quadrant or semicircle (as required), and welded into the corners of cellules (see Fig. 7). The bracing wires are looped round these attachments, doubling back upon themselves (see Fig. 7), thus functioning as a single wire of double length. Splices are dispensed with, but beyond that nothing good can be seen in this method of wiring, which is heavy and very weak, as its " fixing strength " is that of a wire doubled round a small diameter pin in place of twice that strength, as is obtained by splicing.

The use of welding in the building up of the fuselage also appears to be a weak feature. Vibration and reversal of stress cannot be taken adequately by such a structure. The corner attachments are somewhat reminiscent of the well known Short U-bolt. The U-bolt had the standardization advantages of the Fokker fitting, and, in addition, without further sacrifice in weight, was a far more reliable and robust wiring attachment.

FOKKER TRIPLANE.
No. G.125.

Fig. 1.

Fig. 2.

Fig. 3.

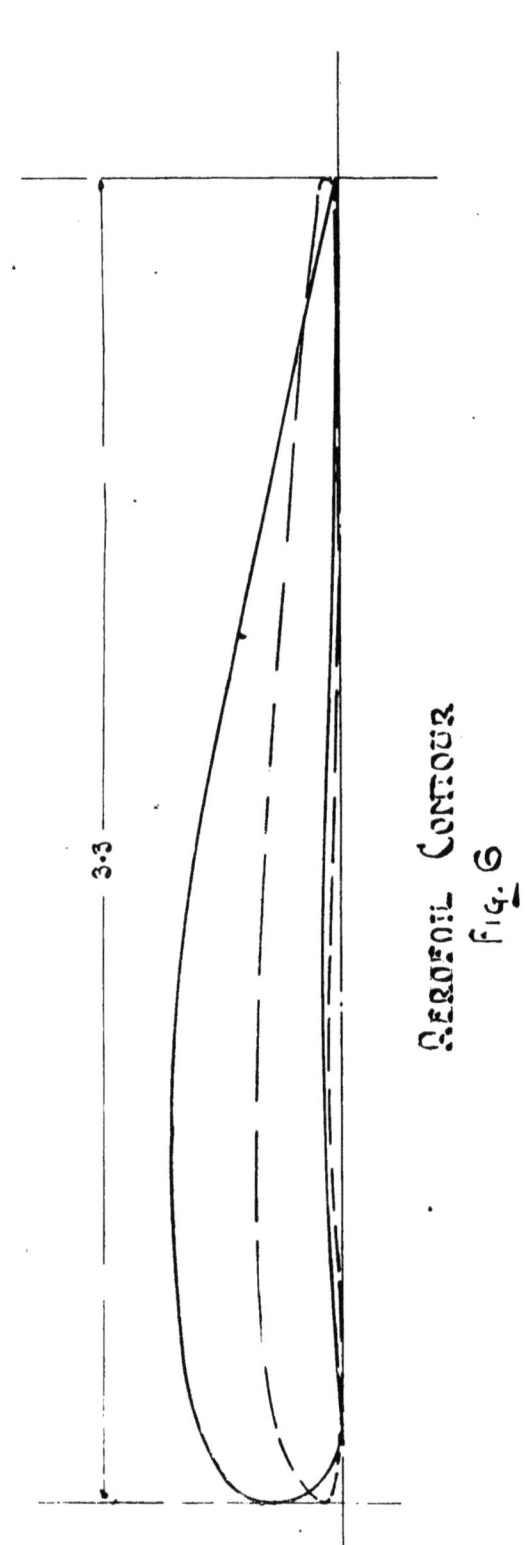

AEROFOIL CONTOUR
Fig. 6

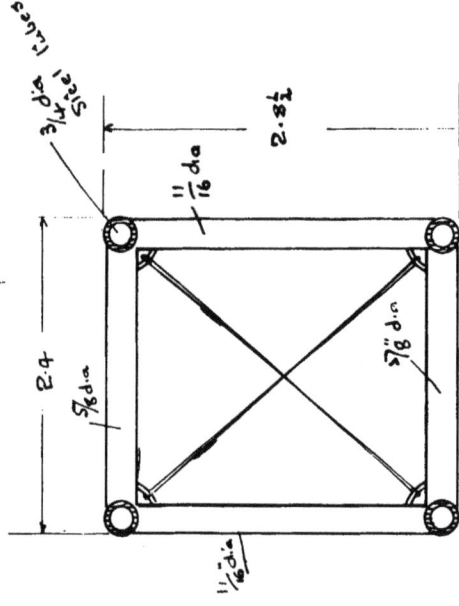

SECTION OF FUSELAGE.
Fig. 7.

FOKKER TRIPLANE.
G.125.

SUMMARY OF CONSTRUCTIONAL CRITICISM.

On broad lines little good can be said of the Fokker structure. The designer appears to have employed considerable ingenuity (or exhibited considerable mental slackness) in devising schemes whereby slight increase of manufacturing speed has been purchased at the price of grave structural weakness or increased weight. Where speed of production has not tempted him, his aim has been reduction of resistance. Here also, strength—and above all, permanence of structural rigidity—has been disregarded, and yet it is hard to see what notable gain of "fineness" has been attained.

WING TIP SKIDS.

These are rigidly-fixed ash skids located under the wing struts. The reason for fitting them is obscure, as they can only come into play as a result of an appallingly poor landing, and if they did come into play, would certainly buckle the flimsy interplane struts.

AERODYNAMICAL FEATURES.

Certain of these features have been mentioned already. In this respect also, the design shows evidence that it has been carried out hastily and in a slovenly manner. There are signs of considerable ingenuity, but they are often marred by lack of broad consideration.

WING DESIGN.

Here, for instance, we have the elimination of external wiring. The "wireless" machine is not a new idea; many constructors have realised its good points, namely, the saving of wire resistance, and the diminution of tuning-up troubles. The Fokker designer has missed the counterbalancing defects, and his method of attack has led him into two grave faults. In the first place, the cantilever construction adopted is not only weak, but essentially non-rigid. The deformation under manœuvring stresses and the consequent variations of aerodynamical load-distribution would appear to render the problem of controllability curiously complicated.

Further, the high cambered section of the aerofoils cannot but counteract the slight advantage due to the saving of wire resistance. Experience has shown that "low lift" aerofoils cannot be beaten for use on scouts, and that whatever advantage in climb and altitude-flying capacity may be attained by the use of "high lift" sections is cancelled and far more than cancelled by the excessive horsepower required at fine angles of attack. When one considers the triplane effect (especially on small gap) which must, from first principles, obtain with such a deeply-cambered section the inefficiency of the main planes becomes evident.

Fig. 6 shows the amazing contrast between the Fokker section (full line) and R.A.F.13 (dotted line), which may be taken as typical of British practice for similar machines.

CONTROLS.

All control surfaces are balanced, but the method of balancing is inferior to that employed on the Albatros.

Ailerons are fitted to the top plane only, a type of construction which has been shewn to be inefficient.

ENGINE.

The Agricultural Hall machine has no engine, but information received from overseas states that the engine is an Oberursel, very similar to the 110 H.P. Le Rhone. In fact, it is understood the only differences are slight points of detail design, and the relative poverty of general finish. For instance, the nose piece is in two portions, the propeller shaft being separate from and bolted to the front plate of the engine.

The carburetter is a French-made Tampier bloctube, presumably obtained from a captured machine.

The oil pump appears to be a German copy of the standard Le Rhone oil pump.

The magneto is a Bosch.

ARMAMENT.

Two Spandau guns are fitted, firing forward through the propeller, and fitted with synchronising gear of the direct flexible drive type, a pinion of the flex shafting engaging with the gear wheel which meshes with the magneto and oil pump drives.

The guns are controlled by Bowden wires, from thumb-pushes on the control lever. Three pushes are fitted, two for firing the guns independently, and the third for simultaneous control.

DIMENSIONS AND DATA.

(CERTAIN DIMENSIONS ARE ALSO SHOWN IN THE FIGS.)

IDENTIFICATION MARKS.

R.F.C. No. G.125.
Maker No. 1856.
Military No. FOK. D.R.1 144/17.
Date of construction, 20/10/17.

WEIGHTS (as stencilled on Machine).

Weight, empty .... 376 kg. = 829 lbs.
Permissible load (including fuel) 195 kg. = 430 lbs.
Total weight .... 571 kg. = 1259 lbs.

WEIGHT OF ENGINE.

334 lbs., including hub, magneto, oil pump and carburetter.   (NOTE:—Weight of 110 H.P. Le Rhone is 330 lbs.)

TANK CAPACITY.

Petrol, 16 gallons } approximate.
Oil, 4 gallons
(approximate duration—2½ hours at 10,000 feet).

From the above it is possible to construct the following approximate weight analysis:—

Fuel, oil and tank .... 170 lbs. (allowing tank 18 lbs.).
Crew .... 180 lbs.
Military load .... 98 lbs.
Engine and propeller .... 358 lbs. (allowing propeller 24 lbs.).
Structure .... 453 lbs. (including engine bearers and instruments).
Structure percentage 36
Surface of main planes—205 sq. ft. (approximately).
Estimated B.H.P. (by analogy with 110 H.P. Le Rhone)—113.
   lbs. per sq. foot.— 6.14.
   lbs. per B.H.P.—11.15.

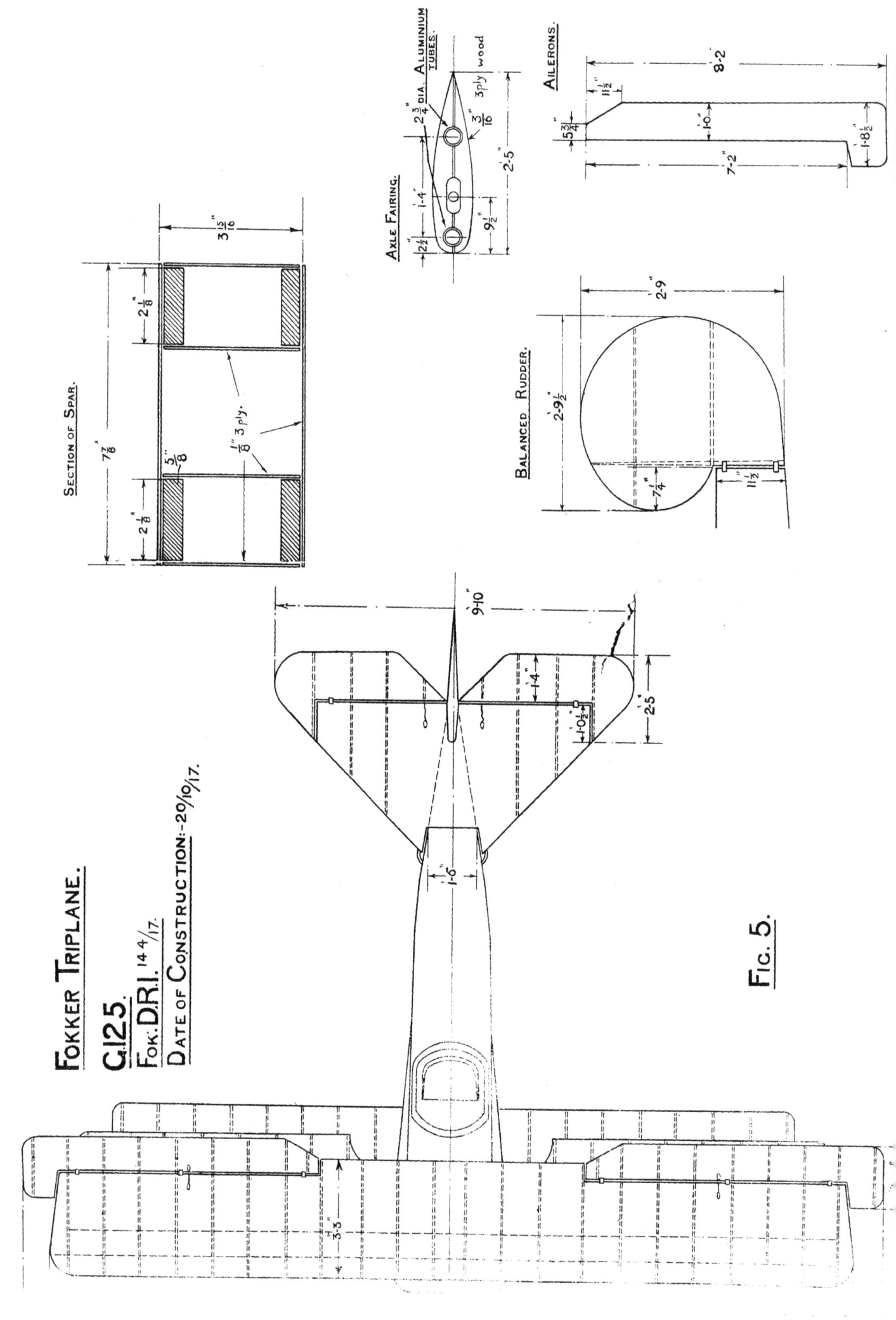

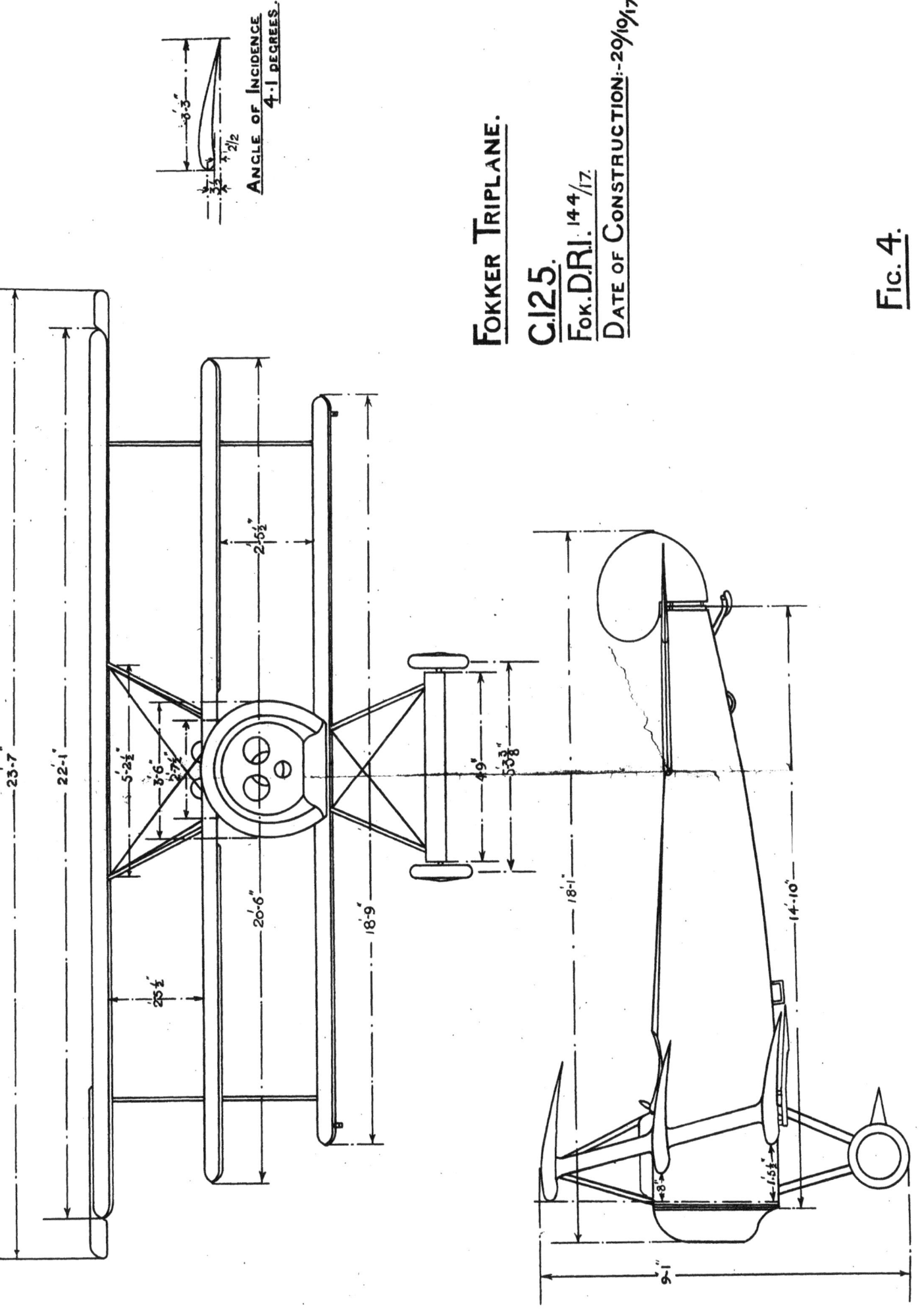

www.ingramcontent.com/pod-product-compliance
Ingram Content Group UK Ltd.
Pitfield, Milton Keynes, MK11 3LW, UK
UKHW051526180426
11947UKWH00019B/1592